CONTENTS

MW01536967

IN MY OWN WAY

By- Eric Stahley

"On January 24, 2019 I jumped in full body and soul into a new world, a new thought process and new me. This day marked a trans-formational shift unprecedented before in my life. This was the official day I stood up to myself, I agreed I was worthy, I was safe, and I was terrified."- E.C.Stahley

THIS BOOK
BELONGS TO

I will gift this book to

PROLOGUE

See, up until this point, I was in agreement with all the things that I couldn't control, and every minute of my life leading up to this moment was taking my health, my mind and my soul.

This is my story, as I wrote it through my physical and emotional transformation. I had been using methamphetamine as a food replacement for the better part of 18 months, up to this moment. With the exception of 20 of the most magnificent months in a relationship, I turned to meth to harvest my artificial soul. To self-medicate and feed my shadow. I used it to enhance my behavioral conditions, I hid behind it, it was my storm, fueling fear. The fear of my shame and what I wanted you to believe about me.

It was familiar, and when my world truly turned upside down in separation and divorce, using methamphetamine was like getting back on a bicycle... I swore I needed it, while I searched for answers, validation and the will to get up.

I am here today writing this because I was in my own way, I did it all in my own way and **In My Own Way**, and I hope to touch just one of you.

MY STORY

*"Hello and welcome
to my story"*

I f you are reading this, and perhaps have chosen
to follow this blog, you must accept and trust
the core ideas of you are "NEVER" alone. As the
owner of my shadow, my spirit, my soul, my heart
and my mind, I am accountable and responsible for
ALL experiences, thoughts, ideas, words, actions,
consequences and results of all that I am capable of.
I am going to share it all, my deepest darkest side
along with the luminous light that radiates from
within to validate not only the core idea of "You are
Never Alone" but also describe the indisputable fact
that there is "Freedom in my Truth".

I am terrified, yet empowered to embark on this
part of my process, to water the foundation of my
spiritual and physical growth...

However, we are programmed and are misguided by what others see, say, do and think based on their fundamental character, beliefs and agreements.

Side note, the Book titled "The Four Agreements" by author Don Miguel Ruiz literally saved my life, quieted my mind, and allowed my perspective and core beliefs to shift into new, healthier and much more comfortable thoughts within myself. I highly recommend it, as well as I am forever grateful to the woman who insisted I kept it in my possession, to ensure the opportunity for me to experience the positive change withheld within its pages.

Today is Thursday January 24, 2019, and starting tomorrow, as I lay my head to rest for the night, I have chosen to engage in a 90 day experiment of sobriety, from it all, whether or not I deem certain things a problem or not.

Other than ibuprofen for the occasional migraine, I will not be ingesting the following for the next 90 days:

(Alcohol)

(Medical Marijuana) which I am a legal card carrying citizen as recognized at the state level

(Methamphetamine)

Now an insight to my brain, mind and spirit...

I am terrified, NO! You are empowered, be the best

you can nurture, wait I can't, no no no, what will my children think, nope, you are not worthy, suffer and perish in your secrets and your darkness, you failure, society thinks you are worthless, your ex-wife and family will crucify you, but wait, what if?...

It hurts, I am scared, I don't want to die!

I don't want to hurt others with my problems, I wish this on no one, and therefore I must accept the consequences up to and including death

There is no one to save me

Nobody cares enough to notice my chemical dependency, society beats into my head addiction is evil...

Did I mention I also suffer from anxiety and depression?...

Raised by a narcissistic mother? Raised by a father who was emotionally and verbally beaten throughout his upbringing?

"My whole life I committed to do EVERYTHING opposite my parents..."

"Since my separation and divorce 5 years ago, I made the choice to go to counselling..."

Where I was introduced to this thing called sense of self, self-love, well-being and self-nurturing...

It's been a process!

A process I wouldn't exchange for anything, a process I wished I had learned as a child... A process that luckily prior to embarking on I was able to teach and help instill within my children purely by doing it opposite than it was done to me...

A process that clearly has revealed an undeniable and uncontrollable truth:

"There is freedom in my truth..."

I will deliberately use this space to tell my story while logging the process of achieving sobriety, recovery, and awareness to all that seek to know that "You are NEVER alone".

The days leading up to this day were terrifying. SO many lies, half-truths, guilt, OH MY the guilt... Self-care starts with acceptance, surrender, forgiveness and faith, IN YOUR SELF.

THIS IS IT

Friday, January 25, 2019. I committed to facing physical detoxification, by myself, no doctors, no treatment center, no counter-active drugs or supervision. In 1991 I was admitted to the McDonalds Center at Scripps Ranch in San Diego California. This was the first time I experienced detox. The Second time, in 1993 at the Freedom Ranch, just one and a half years before moving to Arizona.

These were my accounts of my newly chosen transformation:

This is it

01/25/2019, this is it. Freedom in my truth...

Its magnificent how the universe conspires to light the path of one's intention and desire.

It is equally as magnificent the power we all have...

The reality of our capabilities as a result of such

magnificent power is astonishing.

Faith is a powerful experience!

There is freedom in loving and accepting your darkness!

We are an earth full of individuals, each of us unique, that's ok.

I have manifested remarkable things in my life; I am more than capable of negativity, living in the victim mentality, blame, and judgement

My journey helped me to accept and nurture the natural empathy **"I have for all humans into nurturing myself."**

Ultimately what got me here today was an astonishing quest to fully grasp how I am capable of loving others unconditionally, how my love and acceptance and encouragement of others has been a foundation of my life since I can remember, yet equally being capable of betraying the ones I loved so completely...

I was hurt throughout my life, I gave myself one mission, one thing to accomplish in my life when I was eight years old, and that was to make it a priority to never hurt my loved ones like I had been hurt.

"I Failed"

I raised my children opposite the way I was raised,

to not believe in failure, to not limit themselves with can or can't, success or failure, I have always believed to encourage trying anything and everything, you can never fail...

Last week I told each of my daughters another truth, a disappointing truth; I honored them and thanked them for trusting in me, for believing in my words and lessons, despite their father being 100% guilty of "Do as I say, not as I do"

I have spent my life in service, my mission to spread love...

Why does it hurt so bad...

I was too afraid to practice what I preached...

I found myself in all the darkness, I am responsible and accountable for the pain I've caused and have endured

"This is it..."

Here we go

Reflection:

This was my first night "clean" in over 18 months. My whole routine, everything I deemed safe, normal and "OK", out the window. I had tried to stay clean for a weekend and the next week several times over the last two years, yet always found myself out on Sunday getting more medicine, of all types.

I was TERRIFIED. Yet, I had never been so sure of myself. I threw the flotation device out to myself, and just before I was fully under water, I found my purpose,

I found me...

January 25, 2019 Continued

In this moment, despite the tears and memories, I fully realize how grateful and relieved I am that I wrote all this down publicly! I knew the only way I could help others, to genuinely be in service, to be a good example, to potentially spread my love and intention properly was to apply it first to **myself...**

The light would not be resisted any longer, and my mind had to concede to my spirit, it was a moral imperative...

January 25, 2019 Continued:

Quick check in and WOW

I was choosing to take a moment to acknowledge how magnificent and crazy this is for me in this moment, how the enthusiasm and potential that awaits ahead, how this moment and my undeniable awareness that what's best for me is to continue to stay honest with myself, to embrace all the potential change will provide, yet equally the fears and doubts have gathered their troops to test my spirit, a last battle per say, as I am very use to this battle, my darkness knows nothing else but fight or flight, it only knows battle, my enlightening and powerful darkness is uncomfortable with change, doesn't know how to receive acceptance, love and positive action as a result of its foundation, as a result of the way it's been treated

The darkness is familiar, it is fighting, it is pleading its case of secrecy, concealment...

The path is brand new, never been attempted, the path that I have been searching for, that I have had faith in earning the opportunity to discover

I share this because this is the yin and yang of my being, this is what I have been working through since childhood

This is it. I have been here before sans the path. This time the path is here because I surrendered, I am aware, because I am truly in love with myself and all the potential.

I broke the code, the struggle is so worth it, I owe it to myself to be vulnerable with myself, as unfamiliar as it is to truly be tending to my well-being so deliberately, to have just barely scratched the surface of the true miracle of the love that is my internal spark, to be experiencing first hand just how special unconditional love and acceptance and encouragement feels placed onto myself, magnificent.

Terrifying

What makes it different this time? Why now do I deserve this, how do I know I haven't just manipulated myself, why am I so certain, why and how is it that I give a shit about me?...

I worked my ass off, there are no excuses, I have faced and proven the simple fact of "sense of self"

I did what I had to do to prove it all, I punished myself for hurting others, and I've lived long enough in regret and sadness. I hyper focused on all that is me to truly understand my responsibility, my accountability, I have forced myself to suffer because in those moments I felt I deserved it.

"People have believed in me, people have loved me, people have sacrificed to try and open my eyes to the miracle that is me..."

I hurt these people, and the hurt I experienced as a result motivated me to understand how I could cause such chaos, inconsistency and discomfort, how I accepted losing everything that was important to me, I stimulated my defeated physical body to continue my quest for how.

How do I merge black and white? How do I display and radiate the energy I feel inside outward.

Who or what will or can fix me...

Why am I not getting it...

Why am I so capable of encouraging others yet I continue to hurt and search inside...

Will someone forgive me please?!!?

It was such a relief the moment it all clicked...

You cannot give what you cannot receive

My children are the inspirations and examples of my good intentions and are proof that I am capable of positive influence

All to often what we are missing is directly under our nose.

It works, I see the miracle everyday

It's now time to practice what I have taught; it's time to erase this destructive part of my programmed masculinity

My name is Eric, and all that I am, all of my dark and light, its something special, and as I continue to step out of and away from the ashes, the aftermath, the carnage and chaos which I have manifested, I emerge with an understanding, gratitude, an awareness and in complete humility of exactly who I am...

I am proud that I was and am so completely terrified. I am curious, I have a purpose, and I have a new way, I have me. I am Eric. I am the Butterfly King

I am the luckiest man alive, I am grateful for every experience, every second of my life.

I love you all, you are not alone

I love you me, I am here, I will protect you, I love you, and you deserve it. We have the power to heal, we will use it all to stay balanced in our process, we will thank the universe, the Lord, the powers greater than ourselves in all that we do, every day, we will gain strength in gratitude that our body sustained such abuse. We will proudly and truthfully share our story for our own good, for our growth, to ensure that we are tending to our needs and wants in acceptance, unconditionally, in love

"Today I choose to honor myself with forgiveness, and to go all in with sharing the power of sense of self."

Always feeling so lost, so different, so ignorant, so curious, searching for purpose, wanting to make a difference.

I am grateful to everyone that may or may not relate to my struggles, my process, to the ones that will never get it, to the ones that just had the instinct or whatever to preserve and protect themselves, and especially to the one that may find freedom and hope in similarities in my story and their shadow, I welcome all of your opinions and feedback, and YO, you there who thinks they are unworthy, thinks their dark defines them and is to scary or too dark to be accepted, I am here to tell you, you have not failed, you have not made decisions that warrant your torture, your sadness, what scares you the most holds the potential of your greatest accomplishments, its dark, you may not see it, however you are standing at the entrance to abundance, to forgiveness, to acceptance and all you have to do is turn that handle in faith, and you will find support, you will be empowered, you will be hesitant, you will be scared, you will second guess yourself, you will learn ways to distract from the battle within, like me, in my reality, of recognizing how hard it is to truly change

I will do this, I will resist and I will use every tool I have to get through the next 48 hours of physical transformation, I will not submit to safety of familiarity, I am ready to defeat you artificial soul, your self-created demons are no longer welcome, thank you for your service and your lessons, make it as hard or as gentle as it will be, but trust me motherfucker, I have gotten through way worse things, and every moment of the process I endure in your exit of my body will bring me one moment closer truly being free.

You have been defeated, my freedom lies within my truth, bring it on, game over, goodbye.

Reflection:

The next 24 hours were crucial. These were the

hours I left behind when I first starting using again in 2013. Oh yeah, did I mention I was clean for 20 years prior to all of this?

Nonetheless, in these moments I had only been free from the habit of using for 24 hours, the detoxification was just now making its presence known.

I am a sensitive person. I am a master in my feminine. My first poem I wrote this year, somewhere around April 2019, inspired by my soul brother, read:

"A Master in my Feminine
My light attracts its twin
An infant in my masculine
A spark deep within..."

Thank you Matt, you are my soul brother, legit.

Here are my writings from Saturday January 26, 2019

IT'S ALL GOOD

Good morning

An hour ago I would have said all was good...

It's still all good!

I play hockey, I'm a goalie, I love the sport, I started when I was 40!

It's all-star weekend in the NHL, I think it's the first time I've watched it.

I'm a super emotional person, I feel everything!

How a grown man can sob in happiness for others accomplishments and feel how special their moments can be is sensational.

I however have gotten too sobby.

"BRB goalie skills on now!"

I found Hockey when I was 40 years old, I had never ice skated with the exception of a special friend's birthday when I was 15, to which I put my skates on the ice, fell flat on my back, and retreated to the bench for the rest of the event... ha ha, at 40 NOTH-

ING was stopping me

Saturday January 25, 2019 Continued..

"That was awesome"

Fleury gets out of the crease, takes a picture with a young boy and his father as they are on the other side of the glass, then Fleury hands his goalie stick over the glass to the boy

So rad, thanks Andre for pulling my heartstrings!

Congratulations to the King, Hendrick Lundquist on his 12 shot save streak!

My body isn't sore at the moment, usually my kidneys are killing me, I guess that shift I made last week to drink "Tang" for vitamin C and most importantly because it has more water than soda in it may have helped

I'm horrible at drinking water, unless it's practice or game day.

I'm ridiculously emotional as expected; this is the place that's real!

This is truly How I feel about me, heavy, sluggish, sad.

Thankfully it's different this time, I stepped into my truth!

I have no reason to feel this way, that's why I'm alone.

"I'm taking strength from my greatest weaknesses,

I am now proud from my greatest defeats."

I wish I didn't hurt people,

I'm so sorry for not feeling about myself the way you all did.

It's from you soulmate, it's from you twin flame, my children especially, you all will never know how our memories and experiences are the foundation of sense of self.

I have mistreated you all and it made me a hypocrite.

I now truly understand how deeply and personally I hurt all of you, and I'm so sorry.

But I've proven I'm not my mother, and I have remorse, and the only way to ensure it never happens again, because trust me, I know how I've defended each of your honors because of my stance and beliefs about women and how douche bag men can be, yet I'm guilty of being that guy...

The longest punishment, I inflicted on myself, and that's exactly the reason that sorry doesn't cut it.

My mom is a narcissist. It's pathological not behavioral, meaning she has no idea the monster she is, yet she'll take it so personally to hear that.

She's my mom, I love her, but I don't have the type of mom most of you experienced.

I was awful to my ex-wife during our separation and divorce, inexcusable, last night as my eyes started burning and I could feel the start of the physical separation, and the scatter brained dropped like a mic on a stage, along with a culmination of thoughts and realizations leading up to last night, I began to realize so many things...

My parents divorced when I was 16, I may or may not go back to where this all started, but probably will since writing has been making this process bearable

Despite the tears, I don't necessarily want to experience the real raw feelings again of how I hurt so many, but I owe it to them and to myself. Freedom lies on the other side of this...

Last night I realized despite how badly I've damaged things, we've all been on the same page!

"I've frustrated so many people, including myself"

More fuel that delivers me here today.

I'm the reason we don't co-parent, WTG Dad.

"Last night as I started to drift away from the false reality I've created and I saw a moment of my life plan..."

Now, understanding this was during like my biggest duh doorbell moment, nonetheless I am clear in exactly what I interpreted...

It seems, to a degree, I've been planning for this moment my whole life...

First memory- "I promise to find a mother for my children unlike the one I have."

Second memory, 8 years old, hello sister, omg, I will protect you from this...

Thank god for her, up to that point in my life I was completely isolated other than school and I knew my cousin and his parents.

But I've never really said out loud how in that moment I took responsibility for her, the first thing I taught her, by example, was the power of the middle finger.

> *"In preschool she got on Santa's lap and flipped him right off..."*

I took the belt for that one...

But I also feel I helped her to a degree to not get so damaged...

"So I thought"

I know it's not my fault and for our ages I did pretty

good but I couldn't protect her from everything.

"And I regret it"

She is my absolute best friend, I've allowed us to not be in contact enough because of my shame, she will never ever know what she means to me, and how inspirational and amazing her and her family are.

"She built a world in truth that's and beautiful, I'm so proud of her!"

My fingers are numb, so more later...

It's all been worth it, I will fulfill the lives of others as I fulfill mine.

Thank you all for enduring the nightmare to help me achieve this awareness.

This has been a team effort, I'm so grateful for all my family and friends

I sense myself here, I almost feel guilty for taking pride from disaster, but it's mine and I should have taken it back in the moments.

"Mirrors, teachers, Coaches, love and truth

Soon today will be in the past..."

Mid-Day:

"Just received a call from an inspirational newer friend, very intuitive, the call was right on time."

I want to go play hockey, but my danglers broken from the last shot I took this recently closed past season.

A season I'm proud to say I experienced through clear eyes

A short season, yet nonetheless the longest string of goaltending I've had in my young career without game missing injury

"The universe guides and protects."

My first season, in my first win, and above that a shootout victory, I fractured a rib without knowing despite knowing exactly when it happened in the shootout.

It was like the third game I'd ever started of my first season, a day I'll never forget, everyone I love and care about the most were there that day, my father, my daughters! The absolute love of my life, her eyes sparked when she looked at me , she is amazing. After the game we had a BBQ at my dad's hotel and swam, my lower left rib area very tender and stiff, it was one of the best Sundays ever apart from championship Sundays with the fam during softball...

I'm off topic, I used to say hockey saved my life, today I say I saved my life choosing hockey, and every human I shared a locker room with and ice and concrete time with were my amazing support system

My second season in another shootout I mistimed and made a rookie move, a very poor poke check on the shooter, he delivered a beautiful shot glove side just above the shoulder to score, while simultaneously powering through the shot which I had committed my entire body to, his left knee drives into my stick shoulder, my left shoulder, instantaneously severing tendons out of my rotator cup (cuff?)

"This one was season ending, surgery, long rehab, and heartbreak surrounded this injury."

My life's circumstances were as always extreme, and I seriously didn't think I could return due to the memories.

This might have been one of the first moments when I turned loss and heartbreak into positive energy, and I did return, the first time way too soon but I don't regret it at all, I skated at an NHL rink that day in 2018, so rad.

My mission through November to the end of December 2018 was simple, don't miss a game, play, improve and don't get hurt

"I also was put back onto the backup list, at my main rink where I started my recent career."

I carry the amazing memories with me onto the ice every time my skates land on it, and I thank everyone involved for their love, attention and time they chose to give me those first two seasons, the only other time in my life I felt true pride were when my daughters were born and how amazing their mother was.

See Eric, you're just as responsible for manifesting amazingness in your life as you are for manifesting discomfort.

"I love you all,

Freedom in my Truth."

HATS AND SUNGLASSES

I have this sweatshirt, hoodie.

As a man I have only a few styling vices!
Sunglasses
Shoes
Watches
Hats
Hoodies

This hoodie has been with me through the best moments of my life.

The story for me is very special, how I got it, where I got it, which was with me, the time of my life, super special hoodie.

I'm super sentimental; the littlest simplest things are so meaningful to me, words and gestures, gifts, moments...

I don't believe I've ever had a woman like put on my jammy shirt in the morning, something I kinda dream about...

However, this sweatshirt was drawn to a special person in my life, like it's so rad that so many pictures this sweatshirt seems to be in most, not worn by me!

It's a little thing, and it makes me feel so good, with the exception of not leaving it with its preferred human, lol.

"I slept with this sweatshirt upon its return, not going to lie, it took me weeks to put it on."

Punctuality has never been my strong suit, **truth!**

I was 45 minutes late to my new warrior training weekend on a Friday night due to work.

I had worn that sweatshirt for the first time that week and for whatever reason the night before that Friday I had fallen asleep in my clothes.

I Woke up late and went straight to work that Friday morning.

I had this bag packed, a backpack I cherish from my step brother..

"Everything I needed for late fall in higher elevation."

When I alerted the staff I would be late, knowing the requirements of being on time that weekend, I honestly was praying I could just reschedule...

Before I knew it the weekend was over, and I was in

my same clothes, as they designed it lol.

During that weekend I faced my reality of amphetamine use, my processes were remarkable...

As the dust settled I realized that hoodie had been with me.

"It was my survival, it served as warmth, a pillow, a valuable piece of clothing, durable, capable and stable."

The realization of how I'd never would have chosen to treat it that way, reality turns into gratitude, safety, in my space that hoodie being with me was much more, it meant I had the blessing of not being alone, I realized how much love and care that hoodie represented.

"The human it really should be with was with me!"

Realizing again how I took something so real and shredded it, with my negative self-image, rather than gracefully acknowledging how even endings center with love...

I now wear that hoodie when I'm down, or most often when I need to feel a sense of pride and magic that hoodie carries within it, this hoodie represents the first time I was able to recognize the good and the situation truly evolving out of a hurtful moment, a moment I dishonored by shadow and negative self-image. I speak of a breakup that I handled in the depths of my wounds and self-image, in this new moment of realization of good, I was able to be aware of our breakup truly being in the best interest of us all and our children...

I really didn't behave well during that end and for some time after.

That human left me with a hoodie, a part of herself, and it represents the best of her and I, and this was the first time I started to feel good about who I am, this was the shift That opened the space onto myself to start seeing the good in me, my accomplishments, my heart and soul.

"Thankfully this hoodie unlocked the visibility to see and make amends within myself."

"I'm forever grateful to this human for having the courage to tell me I didn't love myself."

And I'm sorry I took it so personally in the moment, my behavior was a result of you being right, and I just had no idea.

"A blessing that will always bring tears as memories flood my mind, but nonetheless I'm proud of you for your courage, thank you."

I broke my own heart.

Desert Princess; "you didn't deserve my shit in those moments following."

You most definitely helped me to be free!

Thank you.

Reflection:

This particular share I wrestled with including in my story. My body still cringes when I think of my behavior. Of course a hoodie can't change a person, however, symbolism and life can. I just want to thank you all for receiving this with me.

"Saturday was a roller coaster, it's Sunday morning":

LIVING LOVE

I'm alive as expected,

truly empowered!

I'm sore and my shoulders ache,

My hearts beating, as the sobs slowly subside.

I've never been so confident in the possibilities,

all by focusing on the work I need to do for me.

The littlest of blessings in the last 48 hours,

*"Peace is replacing chaos and
confidence is replacing fear."*

This is my story, it's just beginning!

**"I will shower this world in love, by simply loving
and believing in myself.**

**Everything and everyone has contributed to my
awareness and freedom."**

I will always regret how I've hurt so many.

I will hold you dear to me as I willingly and truthfully embrace and live in the moments of my miracle, my hope, my peace, in my recovery, in my truth.

"I'm Eric, I suffer from anxiety and depression, chemical dependency and fear of myself."

I spent a lifetime searching for what I already had-

"The magic inside me"

I love you all, thank you to the universe!

It's time for breakfast.

Sunday January 27, 2019
Continued:

"This is us..."

Used to be a Wednesday night affair, date night.

I think we got partially through the first season,

I tried to pick it up January 2018...

There was this moment, a show reference...

"Just like Kevin, there's just never a "good time"

I respectfully agree, and disagree.

"You'll know when it's a good time, and it's my opinion there's no time like the present."

I got through the episode finally that the statement was born from.

This show is super sweet!

Another great memory, and I love watching one when I can.

They leave me in tears, and I'm proud to say that.

"I'm an empath, and I'm not ashamed anymore of it."

I can't express enough how much strength I'm experiencing from every soul that's a part of my life.

Thank you,

I love you!

I'm scared to death to go to work tomorrow,

I've gotten through worse.

I have an amazing support group,

From everyone in the past and right now in this moment.

"Believe in yourself,

be kind.

Everyone around you is fighting their own battle."

Jack Pearson Just said to his son, it's about hearing and seeing the ones you love.

I'll never miss doing that again.

Goodnight.

"It's about Hearing and Seeing the ones you LOVE"
including yourself.

FUCK IT

5:50am:

"Fuck it all"

Fuck this place, its bullshit, I am outta here...

This is exactly how I feel about everything right now.

Fuck sobriety, fuck work, fuck everything, I have to live in what **"my unworthiness has manifested."**

Ugh.

Thank you, I am not a quitter.

But seriously, all momentum feels to have ceased.

Rubber band snaps...

"I am worthy; I am capable of creating the reality and in achieving what I want."

These are the hard days; I just want to crawl into a hole.

The hole doesn't serve me.

I will continue to stand in the newness, despite my infancy.

I will gain strength from all of it, good and bad.

Thank you universe for the opportunity, sanity, and ability to change.

Please conspire with me.

6:36am:

Alone, helpless, ugh.

Its amazing just how quickly we can shift.

Our surroundings are ours to create,

I honestly hate mine, professionally.

Damn it man, this is so hard.

Rubber Band snaps repeatedly... (I am wearing a rubber band on my wrist and snap it each time a negative thought or judgement crosses my mind about me)

Positive thoughts,

I am worth it

I can

I will

I am so sad today

I hate feeling like this

"Put on the face for the world to see"

No time for that during the work day,

I will create the change that I need, immediately.

I can!

Through the tears and frustration and all the feelings of why I should just return to what was normal.

But there is no freedom there,

no triumph,

no peace.

"I can get through this, today and tomorrow."

I am going to have to whine a bit, eventually I will look back and smile at this hardship.

But in this moment I am struggling,

I call on the strength from all of you.

Thank you,

I love you all.

8:15am:

Support

I have support, 13 amazing people with the courage

to be seen and received.

I have an intimate team of two people, who we are committed to supporting each other.

First break is 15 minutes away,

I have made it 1/3 of the way through my toughest day,

I like rubber band snaps.

GOING INWARD

Another Story

I am reluctant to share this story, but I know I need to since it has been captivating my mind all weekend.

"I had an amazing cousin in my life, he was a blessing of a soul. A true mountain man, he was full of love."

In my dry days and when I was a part of a family for the better part of 20 years, my family believed in me, they saw my power, yet I was too ashamed of its birthing place, I was to afraid of the responsibility.

It wasn't the first or the last time I was praised for being the miracle to kick substance abuse.

"I couldn't save him; I couldn't even help, though I tried, because of my self-belief and self-image."

I vowed 3 days ago to never let myself not help anyone with their struggles, if even to just lend an ear.

By choosing to share my story, my recovery, my construction of me, I will ensure I have the opportunity to touch others, while healing myself.

I am rising from my self-image, my negative self-talk, I have chosen to walk into the light of my power by being proud of how my life shook out, being proud of who I am, and being proud at the possibility of touching someone else.

I have been through divorce, I have been through losing true love after divorce, I have been a difficult partner, husband, father, son, brother, and person on this earth.

I honestly learned more about parenting and marriage during my court ordered parenting classes.

This was at one time a very sore subject.

I admit I had nothing but faith and good intention when I embarked on marriage and parenthood.

It is my intention to use my process and experiences to potentially introduce new coaching and perspectives in men's health and awareness. Specifically to those new couples on their path to marriage and children, and also to the men who have found themselves blessed with love a second time, men who recognize their responsibility to themselves, and the power they have as they set the examples to their children and their partners children.

All this in due time, I have work to do for me first, which I will gladly and willingly share here.

In the meantime I highly recommend seeking out Traver Boehm or Shana James, or pop open your podcast app and search for self-help coaching.

If you suffer from any type of mental illness, addictions of any kind, anything, please trust me, you are not alone, there are resources out there, and people like me that want to share and are willing to listen.

These resources helped me to unlock my code, to face my shadow, to continue to share my story in hopes I can reach just one more soul.

"I am not an expert, I am a man who is not afraid to admit he completely and unintentionally fucked up, and I know that it's ok, I have been blessed with the ability and capability and sanity to change, to surrender, to get honest, to cry, and to succeed in enjoying these moments and all to come by living in the freedom of my truth."

With love and Light,

Eric.

Reflection:

In this moment my life has led me to the 12 step program in my teens, I sought alternative treatment when I was a young adult, had spent 20 years clean from methamphetamine and this was day 3 of recovery, again, day one of working in recovery.

I was blessed to be invited into a program that kicked off on January 25, 2019 called Intoxicate. An experiment if you will, as my beloved coaches and friends, Traver H Boehm and Courtney McNabb framed it to be. They simply asked us to give up our vice, whether it be food, alcohol, drugs etc. The purpose to give up your vice for 90 days was simple. To create space for healing. To create space to nurture and develop your highest self and awareness.

For me it was life or death. A moral imperative as I stated earlier. With or without the program.

I begged to get into the program, I didn't have the resources to pay for it...

To this day, I am in contact with most of my program mates, and my mentors and coaches in Traver and Courtney.

Following will describe how this type of support is crucial for anyone of us struggling with anything.

"You are never alone; you are not weak or unworthy for needing and asking for help. Ask. Reach out. There are so many of us out here to walk with you. It is with infinite love I say this to you."

It was the one thing I did that made all the difference... admit and ask for help...

CHASING THE DRAGON

Omg, I have been so tired. I laid down last night at 6pm and pretty much stayed there until the alarms started going off at 4:44am.

"Day 8, this marks the longest time I have been without mind altering chemicals of any sort in my system the last year and a half."

Red Dragons!

Big day today, I am super stressed, yet it is so manageable with the momentum that is gaining.

I do have a story to share, perhaps tonight, about a dream on Saturday night.

It was amazing,

I don't dream so it was rad.

I love you all, any and all of you that have been with me, that are following this, or that just are there!

"WE all have the power to spread love and light in this world."

Sure beats the alternative,

wish me luck on this miraculous day 4.

In love and Light,

Eric.

SPIRITUAL PUNK

*"My wrist is red from posi-
tive affirmations."*

TIRED AF

Momentum...

9:51am:

Spiritual Punk Rock!

I just found out there is a movement in Punk rock, something dear to me, "Youth of Today".

I can't wait to dive into this new found knowledge Noah Levine, Author of "Dharma Punx" - check it out.

"Youth of Today" is a punk group that shifted to spirituality from the stereotypical "Punk Rock" way.

Noah, his book, this realization of a music genre that I so connect to being a part of the journey I call my own, on this day, I needed this.

When I created the Pandora station "Youth of Today" it most definitely didn't disappoint.

"Music has always soothed my soul, however it was the rhythm and beats, I never really heard words."

All of a sudden I was hearing the message in all my musical tastes, like ALL OF THEM.

Pretty rad.

1:09pm

Walk Tall in your Truth

Today has been a rough one, but not the last several hours.

Just when you think you hit the wall, momentum pushes you through... like "Hey Kool Aid" through that wall...

Haha'

Im Kool Aid!

"Support, love, encouragement, from the depths of the forgotten almost, in so many ways, exclaiming my truth continues to unveil the unexpected..."

This little cart is gaining the momentum of a freight train...

Man, I am so blessed.

Thank you all.

In love and Light

Eric

Some Thoughts on February 2019:

February 2019, this was a huge month.
In this month, I had realized you could describe the six or so years leading up to this moment as me being a roller coaster, or storm.

"I made a post describing me as a Tsunami."

The moment I realized I was creating this outwardly storm because I was SO afraid and ashamed of ANYONE seeing me for who I was, especially me seeing me for me, that day was pivotal.

That day helped me to save me, that day got me through being terrified to me being content in this moment.
That was the day that created the space for the storm to pass, for the calm to arrive, for the awareness and education to start that allowed me to weather the stormy day without being the fuel of the storm.

Here we continue to Friday February 1, 2019:

AFFIRMATIONS

Day 6 & 7

Yo!

Day 6 and 7 were mother fuckers!

Day 6 and 7 were miracles,

"Day 6 and 7 stimulated all the feels, the fears, the negative..."

"DAY 6 AND
7 DELIVERED
BLESSINGS,
AFFIRMATIONS
AND HEALING!"

"DAY 6 AND 7 HUMBLE ME"

I'm exhausted; I owe you a story or two.

"I love you Eric Stahley,

You did it!"

Saturday February 2, 2019

THE GIFT

It's still day 8

I delivered a thank you and a small handmade gift, I saw her today.

I highly recommend seeing the movie "Say Anything"

Or Silver Linings.

That's all for today,

You're not a monster- me.

You are love and light,

I love you Eric, even though at times you feel you don't deserve it,

Rubber band snap,

I love you Eric I love you-me.

You're not a monster,

I'm not a monster.

After difficult Day 8, Day 9, February 3, 2019

"Let's go for a ride, shall we?"

12:20am

RAIN DROPS

It's raining,
I haven't slept since day 8.

I was really hoping I wouldn't experience not being able to sleep.

I had hoped I had exhausted my body enough by not sleeping for the last year.

It started last night,

I used to have this "routine "so to speak.

If I behaved well in the week I'd stay up most of Friday night,

After using all week.

Ugh, that truth...

Well last night I was making dinner and realized I was kind of spinning out, yet no real reason.

I recognized this and went to bed,

Knowing we have the power to make habits.

Habits are easy to make, hard to break.

The self-loathing, the self-hate I've cast upon myself my entire life...

This is a habit? Yes

Breakable? Yes

It's really raining, sounds beautiful in this moment.

Like I said I haven't slept yet.

"It is seriously disturbing yet freeing to be wide awake with no reason."

I'm alone with my mind,

did you know the mind and brain are separate?

Think about it, someone recently told me this...

So, I'm all alone with my thoughts, they are in my mind.

My brain controls by basic bodily functions

Freedom

Anyway, I'd be willing to bet most anyone previous to 9 days ago would be super
Concerned about my condition at this moment.

But I'm not using

I'm not drinking

I'm not smoking

I'm thinking, I'm searching, I'm fucking sober yo, and I'm in mother fucking beautiful recovery

Standby please, favorite part of the movie.

1:15am

THE SILVER LINING

Silver Linings.

Such a beautiful movie.

Bradley Cooper, Jennifer Lawrence, seriously, Chris Tucker! Robert De Niro.

Seriously, I wish I could personally thank each and every one of them.

So, I've been alone with my thought.

And I have been watching movies

And I just fully effed up and put on Bruce almighty...

I just signed up for 24 hours of crying lol

Ok I'm avoiding.

Thinking clearly, and being honest with myself,

fuck.

I hid behind my "mental illness " this year to cover my chemical dependency.

I totally deceived myself and others,

why am I able to be aware of this?

Because I chose to "act and be crazy" instead of asking for help.

I was too ashamed to be honest, so I made something small super big!

"I scared people and I scared myself."

I hurt people,

I do have anxiety legit.

And it happens sometimes,

and it's real.

Yet I've been ashamed of that,

when someone that loved me unlike anyone had before, like seriously, she spent days researching.

And she came to help me, vulnerable, serious, in love, in our love, in our light.

"I was so confused and scared, and ashamed after my episode..."

I remember sitting on the floor of our bedroom,

leaned against the closet doors.

"So ashamed, so scared, so confused, so HURT, so defeated."

I was not in the moment

I used to think that once I hurt or disappointed anyone, I could never "fix" it, make up for it, be forgiven...

Forgiveness

I spent 20 years with my soulmate, I hurt her on our wedding day, I held
Back on our kiss, imagine, the best years of my life during those times, my
Beautiful daughters, our beautiful family, her beautiful family, they accepted me.

"Yet scared, living in darkness, constantly worried about when she'd leave.."

Manifest

She left, thank god for her, I begged for forgiveness, but a soul that is empty and dark is,
incapable of being forgiven...

I met my twin flame, my clearest mirror ever.

My back leaned against the closet doors, she wasn't as emotional as me. Her eyes
Puffy, determined, concerned, loving

In the days that followed, I didn't spiral, I dove down that rabbit hole...

And I made sure to hit every millimeter of every edge and rock and darkness.
Of that hole as I beat myself up for what? A medical condition? For her unconditional
Want and desire to help me, us?

1:46am

In the days that followed I dove down the rabbit hole,

every millimeter of that hole of darkness a complete beating,
Of myself, for something I can't control,

Did I mention she wanted to help me, us?

The moral of this all:

**"We are powerful, our minds a bridge to the divine, to the primal,
They are the vibration that connects us all."**

Connects us to the universe,

our thoughts are powerful.

Mindfulness is key, **SELF LOVE IS ESSENTIAL,**

Self-respect, being present.

You truly cannot receive another person if you haven't received your self.

I mentioned a few days ago this was the hardest work.

I'm truly sorry to everyone,

i'm truly sorry to myself.

These last 72 hours have been a mother fucker,

yet they also have opened up space and awareness.

I'm struggling with forgiving myself,

this is truth,

I fucked up.

But I'm here, and there is freedom in my truth.

My best self, the example I have always intended, it starts inside me.
It starts with loving me, treating me the way I positively treated others.

"It starts with forgiveness."

My coaches are my heroes, my team; Love Warrior's my rock, my program mates.
"My strength, my mentors, my savior."

My kitten, well, I'm scared of her, jk, well a little hahaa.

In this movie, Bruce Almighty, Morgan Freeman is god

As he is fixing the (lights) and walking down the ladder, he says-

"It's pretty bright, too bright for most, as they spend their lives in the dark, afraid of the light "

Or something like that,

guilty as charged..

I'm aware I've manifested, fed, remodeled, 100% lived, preferred and
Encouraged my shadow and darkness.

"Afraid of the light"

Funny thing, I prefer the light, as in the sun, my body needs it!

"Funny thing is, no matter how filthy something gets, it can always be cleaned right up"

In love and light

I love you me

Eric

Reflection:

I have re-written, started over, and re-framed this book like a half a dozen times. Stimulating, am I right? I am choosing to deliver my story in its true and raw form. I do understand it can be, well, not a flowing read for you all.

I am also certain that if you are still with me, it's because it has in some way captured your attention and interest.

I would say you probably "Feel Me" in some regard.

"I am hoping, in this moment, you are lost in my story."

A few more personal blog shares then a conclusion...

MY FELLOW HUMANS

Quick check in :)

This universe, my fellow humans!

I did it different, shared this blog with a new friend.

I was blessed with a response of "You write so beautifully"

Blessings, big and small, all around us.

In love and light

M**e**

FORGIVENESS IN ACTION

Forgiveness in Action

I have realized there is forgiveness in action, in service, in service to one's self.

She says I write beautifully, says I am a cool guy.

She knows me exactly in this moment, she knows me completely, she knows me as these words have described.

"She knows me as I know myself, honest, truthful, determined, terrified."

We know each other, my intensity not a bad way, it's been easy because it's real, truthful, vulnerable, I see her and I know she sees me.

She told me recently that change is hard, but once you get going it's a piece of cake! :)

Cake, yum, sounds good!

It is a little uncomfortable for me to say this, but it

is also super rewarding, as well as freeing.

"I am in love with myself, like I feel like I do when I am in love with someone or something."

This guy is feeling super free; I continue to build momentum, thanks to so many, thanks to myself.

I took a chance on myself by sharing my story, by being fully legit with myself, with my shadow, with my darkness, with sharing everything that once shamed me, scared me, the stuff I used to think I was only worthy of.

I put a lot of positive changes for me in motion before meeting this special friend.

She inspires me :)

I am so blessed, and I am glad I took the chance to introduce me to her, to you all, to myself, to my group and my Love Warrior Team, and last but not least, my two beautiful coaches.

I am finally making positive changes for myself, as scary as they are, and I am being rewarded and reminded daily why this is the way, so many special people in my world, so much support, so much love...

This love affair with myself is so rewarding, its challenging and it is terrifying a lot of the time.

But I look into the mirror, give myself a smirk, say "I love you Eric" and walk each day in humility, gratefulness and appreciation of this life I have been granted, and I take great pride in taking on the endeavor of doing the work, for doing it the opposite of how I know it to be.

"This small practice is rewarding me with true love, and allowing me to share it as I intend, because I have found the intimacy and power in loving myself. Even when I feel weird about it..."

There is freedom in service, and service returns the opportunity of forgiveness of me, in acceptance of all that I am, in my freedom to introduce myself to me, and you all.

In love and Light,

Me

ASS KICKER

Happy day 14!

I know today is going to be the hardest day for me to date…. a guaranteed ass kicker that started last night ,with news .

We are learning how to face our challenges in new ways, right?!

Rubber band fucking snap yo's…

I am so blessed to have you all in "my corner"

Cheers to the tears and the challenges!

There is a positive buried in every negative, I know this.

I stand up tall today despite the possibilities,

I am proud of myself, of you all.

I am sad,

and I am scared.

"But I have momentum and strength from us all and our Heavenly Father and universe, as well as 8 and 15 year old Eric, those two guys are being

brave."

In love and light

Me

Reflection:

Having support is key. Our Coach, Courtney McNabb in our Intoxicate program, led me down 2 different shame meditations, over the phone, yet I felt her presence with me, literally her hand holding mine, she promised she was with me and would stay with me.

"Tears rolling down my face in this moment as I re-call these experiences, they were so powerful."

These were the moments I got to go back, and truly start the forgiveness process within myself, with support, safety, and most importantly without judgement.

"There are so many ways for us to access our trauma, find the one that works for you, pursue it, feel it, endure it and conquer it, with compassion and forgiveness and acceptance. I can promise, it will change your life!"

This is how I can state that 8 and 15 year old Eric are being brave, these are the two boys that were left behind with no explanation, these boys now know this man will never leave them behind or shame them again, only encouragement and acceptance and love will they endure for the duration of this magnificent life.

Reflection:

5:13pm, I found myself moving major emotion and memories through my body.

Yo

 "Every tear has a purpose, but not every purpose deserves a tear." - Eric Stahley

6:28pm

Friday, February 8, 2019

Ass kicking Day 14, Victory

Last night I found out the Yavapai County Constable had stopped by my work with papers...

This is what led to the positive conversation with my ex-wife, as I contacted her to let her know the sheriff was trying to serve me.

I told her I thought it was a restraining order from my ex-girlfriend.

Last Saturday I dropped off a picture frame I made her and a thank you card, my ex-girlfriend is the one who introduced me to my coach, Traver Boehm.

She asked me to leave 9 days after I had experienced full reconstruction surgery on my left shoulder, three days prior to Thanksgiving 2017.

Being a lawful, terrified and sad citizen today after 8 phone calls, two messages and an email I went to the sheriff's station.

Constable Williams' Office was next door, after being told he was off today the very nice clerk came out to show me his door, then she knocked, and he answered on his day off.

(They don't call me diligent Eric for nothing)

Introduced myself, asked to shake his hand, apologized, he saw I had been crying all day, I couldn't hide it, I was sure in my gut I was right.

The paperwork was in his car at home...

He put his hand on my shoulder and said
"Son just breathe, it's just a civil matter, no big deal, you're not going to jail".

Jail, how I've avoided jail is a blessing I can't ignore.

I said, I'm in day 14 of recovery and sobriety, sir, and if my gut is correct I bet it's a restraining order".

He said "Eric, that's a good bet".

Is it ok if I stop by your work Monday? Or if not I can meet you somewhere else, work is the only address I had.

"I said no sir I have nothing to hide or be ashamed of, my freedom is in my truth".

He shook my hand and I walked away,

"ass kicker of a day."

I made amends, showed gratitude and appreciation, and it resulted in a restraining order.

Red dragons

Cheers to the tears and challenges,

I then did some homework.

Drove to Sedona, dropped a small gift off to a friend, enjoyed the beautiful world we live in.

And stepped away from this challenge,

on my way home this ticker tape went through my mind.

"Every Tear has a purpose, but not every purpose deserves a tear,

Stay strong all of you, I love you,

I leaned on us hard and furiously today. "

I apologize to Courtney McNabb and Traver H. Boehm and the rest of you if I over posted today.

I used EVERY tool and resource and lesson at my disposal today to ensure a positive, healing and growth of an experience and outcome.

Thank you all, I love you, I needed each and every

one of you today and you were all there, I'm beyond grateful .

In love, light and exhaustion.

Goodnight

Eric Stahley

Reflection:

In This exact moment, the song "Ride" by Twenty One Piolets is playing in my apartment.

That is significant because that song was popular during my time with her. The kids and her would sing it, they all had such beautiful voices, the youngest, so dear to me, he sung it with purpose!

I have spoken about my behavior during our breakup throughout this story, and again, it was inexcusable.

"However, I can be remorseful and can accept it as a beautiful part of me, despite the tears."

The papers, as my coach explained on group call during the Intoxicate program, were a strong, valid and necessary statement of the space she required, which I had not given her despite her multiple requests.

My best friend, my legit homie, I couldn't honor her in my shadow. Regretful for my actions I shall always be....

After a semi quiet weekend, Day 17 presented itself, here are my words.

KINDNESS IS KEY

Random acts of kindness and insecurity. Snowed again last night!

I ate shit walking down the driveway,

as I drive onto the highway I was pulled over

The sheriff pulled me over to alert me my brake lights were covered in snow, he brushed them off and sent me on my way.

How kind was that? :)

"My mind is in overdrive today, I have found myself worried a bit..."

No big deal, insecurities are healthy IMHO

Yet, a bit much sometimes.

Feeling good, Day 17

I love you,

Me

Reflection:

Late on this Monday afternoon I was presented at work with a mistake I made. It triggered me fully. Yet, this trigger was screaming from an authentic place. The President and Vice President of the company I am working for in that moment are true friends whom I respect and love. However, complete and total change and transformation was imminent, and while I feel my actions implied they were responsible for the decisions I made next, my motivations and necessity to rock my own world were all mine. I will always appreciate and love them for all they endured and encouraged me in my professional time with them.

LEAVE THE PAST BEHIND

FREEDOM

Never again will I hold myself back from what's best for me!

Ok peeps, I JUST QUIT MY JOB!
I'm totally ok, it was extremely toxic, I realized after Sunday no amount of money or security is worth my safety, health, sanity and sobriety.

NOTHING

I'm getting cleaned up and off into the world.

I love you all!

One of my dearest friends once told me "You don't give notice to a job you never intend on returning to".

In this case, against all of my professional integrity and reputation, I heeded this advice.

"It hurt, yet it was SO right for my soul."

Not because of them, it was right for me.

Reflection:

I spent the next 3 days driving the state of Arizona delivering bound copies of my resume.

It was in these moments, I became aware that I was going to become an author.

"These were the moments I was gaining realization of starting my movement "Go All In for YOU."

These were pure moments of faith, and faith is magnificent!

I was engaging the freedom of living in my truth,

and I was absolutely terrified...

The next entries describe some of the work I was doing to connect with me, to identify shame, to lean into resistance and the emotion in lieu of medicating from it...

I AM WORTH IT

My shame timeline is extensive, this work is deep, dark, rewarding and freeing. 5 journals from December 2013-present day February 17, 2019. Dark angry resentful words in the beginning, repetitive lessons logged in different experiences throughout the years, devastating words of self-loathing and hate, unworthiness, long entries detailing why I must die, a restraining order with text messages of threatened suicide, of how my girls wouldn't even come to my service dated as recent as early 2018, all sprinkled with the miracles I've experienced as well.

I had to break my shame timeline down to yearly contents, a PDF I can't seem to attach.

A short but deliberate voice memo in tears, yet in strength simply stating "Eric, you have nothing to be ashamed of EVER AGAIN (SHOUTING)...

My shame is a black quicksand that starts in my heart and rapidly consumes my entire being, yet, my light and purpose is an equally powerful radiant strong and diligent sensation that quickly dissolves

this black quicksand, and 12 year old Eric puts on a new pair of pants and is now playing... in the light
My meditations this week found me giggling, enjoying and playing in the moment.
Thank you Courtney McNabb for walking with me through this journey.
I'm so proud of you all, thank you for lending me your strength and courage this past week and 23 days!

I am love I am the light I am worthy! This is fucking hard ass shit yo's.

I love you all, my dear friends and family,

thank you for allowing me to share!- Eric

A NEW FOUNDATION

Saturday February 23, 2019 - My "3rd" Lifetime 30 Day Milestone.

Day 30

I miss them; I miss the "us".

No, not talking about drugs, I'm talking about my partners, my best friends.

Especially her, my closest friend.

This life is something else, even when you are doing all the right things, you still are capable of hurting others, disappointment etc.

I am pretty sure she knows I didn't intend for either of us to experience such swift change.

I respect her for pulling away, and I hope she knows how much I care for her, appreciate her, and wish all her dreams to come true.

I hope she realizes no one has accepted or encouraged me like she has.

"Nothing is set in stone, tomorrow is to be determined, the past history."

I hope they all know how I wish things could be different; I know they know each moment is different in the best way.

Resistance appears when we are at the edge of our greatest selves

Difficult or bad things don't happen TO us, they happen FOR us.

I had 20+ years clean before the relapse.

"Cheers to the tears, and to this 30 day milestone."

I CAN FLY

Last week was exciting and challenging in very private personal ways. Last Monday I had a phone interview with a firm in Houston Texas, on Tuesday, my youngest daughter was admitted to the hospital, on Wednesday was my 47th birthday, and on Friday I flew to Houston Texas for an interview and back to Arizona all in the same day. Side note, Northern AZ was experiencing a record breaking snow storm.

This past week I learned about resistance. My entire life I viewed things as "signs". I had just celebrated 30 days of recovery and healing, yet my world had been rocked with my youngest in the hospital and me having to face my very real fear of flying, along with record breaking snow that nearly caused me to miss my flight. (Thank you to my oldest for telling me to leave for the airport NOW on Wednesday).

"30 days prior, I rocked my families world with my news, my daughters and their mother, alerting them all of my relapse and commitment to recovery."

"Resistance"

I accomplished my mission of finding a mother unlike my own for my children. However I also hurt their mom, and myself and them, when I became too consumed with my darkness and wounds to be the man they had always known.

In my writings, I have made several statements of this being a team effort. I have talked about mirrors and unconditional love and support.

It comes in all forms.

News flash people, this may sting, however I am here to tell you, NO ONE has to, or can be legally bound to, or even has to choose to put up with YOUR SHIT. PERIOD. A person definitely can't be forced to.

"Energy is Energy. Intuition is real. Call it what you will. Don't deny yourself in this moment, you know what I mean."

I am going to use an analogy I was taught in regard to integrity. Integrity, that word and the definition I formed for it, is what I tagged as the trigger to my complete breakdown at age 40. However, I didn't have an understanding of integrity...

Imagine Integrity (Also known as your genuine self) as a bag of liquid...

Every secret, every shady move, thought, feeling, action... all of those puncture holes into that bag...

What happens? It eventually bleeds out!

Each hole punctures your authentic and genuine energy, often times the same energy that attracted your wife or ex-girlfriend, or ex-husband or ex-boy-friend.

Each puncture bleeds your light and magnetism, your truth, your integrity.

"Often times these punctures are already there in the form of trauma and wounds."

These punctures affect all of your relationships, friends, family, lovers, however, they especially affect the relationship with **YOURSELF.**

Reflection:

The mother of my children, she has been in my corner through it all, all while I was feeding this world complete bullshit. She doesn't have to like me, but she has, along with her amazing family, afforded me the space to get to this place I am in, and I am forever grateful, because she loves our children unconditionally and genuinely.

Here are my thoughts from Monday February 25, 2019:

Monday, February 25, 2019

FLIP FLOPPING

Hello family!

I received offers from Houston and Sedona this evening.

I want to be completely honest in this moment...

From feeling really focused and content yesterday, I'm experiencing such positive momentum shift into familiar situations and feelings and thoughts of fear, uncertainty, lack of clarity, insecurity and fragility.

I told both companies I'd render my decisions to them by 5pm MST tomorrow.

I have a meeting tomorrow and am anxious and nervous to bring my authentic self, with a focus on my listening ears, and a strong resolve and energy that demonstrates an undeniable statement of it being about her, not me, one that radiates acceptance, encouragement, love and pride of her and her work and courage.

"I will continue to remind myself it's ok to mull all of this over, and that the path will be undeniably revealed to me During or after this session."

I cannot believe how terrifying it is standing before all the greatness I've manifested in such a short amount of time, legit, it's uncomfortable as fuck, but doable.

I love you all

In love and light

Eric

Reflection:

I was blessed to speak to both of my daughters on Tuesday February 26, 2019 in regard to my job opportunities in Sedona AZ and Houston TX.

This story is about healing, change, and awareness.

These conversations were the first in years where I could hear and receive them.

"I truly know that they unconditionally wanted me to do what is best for me."

This is not how I was raised, this is not the norm.

"However, feeling them in their words was so powerful."

On Tuesday, February 26, 2019 I accepted the position in Houston which afforded me a full re-ignition of my career...

On Saturday March 9, 2019 I set off in my 1988

Volkswagen Vanagon packed with everything I deemed necessary, my father following in my other car, to Texas City Texas. 1,667 miles, 2 and a half days, two overnights, and I received the keys to my next chapter on March 11, 2019 at approximately 1pm CDT.

I started work on March 13, 2019.

"I miss my daughters so very much, however, they are young adults, and they both know how much I love and support them, as I know they love and support me."

"Resistance is not happening TO you it's happening FOR you" -Eric B. Hodgson

And It Begins!

MAGNIFICENT

I t is day 48, I had to count, and things have been moving yet standing still at the speed of light.

It's been magnificent; magnificent is a word in my vocabulary that I cherish.

Magnificent can be used to describe it all.

Overall, I have achieved a contentment I've been working to grasp consistently my whole life.

That is magnificent!

Then, there are moments where memories, feelings... emotions...

Instinctual, there are just some things I've experienced that feel like I've carried for lifetimes...

Loneliness, sorrow, regret, anger! Disappointment, regret.

They hit me in one total force of blah, a handful of

special people whom I immediately reflect on..

I miss my daughters so much; I regret my ability to hurt , to disappoint...

That is magnificent!

"Overwhelmed as I type through eyes filled with teardrops, the sea of tears has changed, the tide has a different purpose and meaning..."

I miss her, legitimately, I miss my desert princess and her beautiful family, it's real.

That is magnificent!

However, what I experience in this moment I didn't have a short time ago...

A

Relationship

With

Myself...

That is magnificent!

As we share our abundance, our struggles , in our truth, with others, in any and all of the ways we can...

It's healing,

journaling is healing!

Taking this moment to share my magnificence is

healing,

magnificent is one of my most cherished words in my vocabulary.

It allows me to communicate with contentment...

No matter which magnificent moment I'm in...

In love and light,

Eric

"Go All In For YOU"

A movement I've founded...

All beings are worthy, you are worthy, I am worthy!

Go all in for you!

Today is a day I almost got lost in all the magnificence!

I am blessed to have the courage and the awareness to recognize how easy it is to be jaded
By magnificence, in the positive abundant sense

A part of me told myself I didn't need to do this tonight...

Another example of how magnificent we are within our minds and bodies!

Now my glasses are only a tad fogged, a tad salty on the cheeks.

A magnificent contentment has been restored,

By living in the freedom of my truth.

"You are NEVER alone"

You are never alone, a reflection of my magnificent storm .

THE WAVES

Imagine a tsunami, a magnificent storm; in my interpretation a tsunami storm carries it all, relentless, powerful, destructive...

And that's before the wave...

The waves...

A tsunami has no prejudice, you cannot reason with it, you cannot shift it...

Often we are warned, some of us will stand up tall to it...

The tsunami will be what it is meant to be, it will cause lives to change, it's a force of nature...

Most often leaving pain, loss, destruction in its path...

"Yet it has a purpose, as uncomfortable and destructive and terrifying as it can be, it rises and then it's gone..."

But not forgotten!

It doesn't fix or make up for or serve much other

purpose other than leaving all that experience left behind in its wake...

A tsunami in the way I see it, feel it and interpret its magnificence is a result of a relentless, unexpected fist pounding type of event...

"I realized today my life was the source of what creates a tsunami, the resentment, the fear, the anger, the pain, the hopelessness, the unworthiness..."

Every time I was punished or disciplined or beaten or verbally abused as a result of my spirit, my personality, my actions, my wants, needs or desires from childhood on, every time I did these things to myself in judgement of me especially... I created the force that just continued to push these gigantic, powerful destructive waves outward onto the world, but more significant is how they constantly broke and crashed upon my inner child, my spirit, my soul, my mind...

As they passed in waves or seasons leaving my friends, family and loved ones negatively affected, I inside never had experienced the storm to ever pass, as I pounded harder onto myself as I watched my whole life, everything and everyone around me rebuild as they became more affected by the storm, as they learned to build boundaries, levies and eventually evacuation plans to save themselves as these waves became consistent, spilling out of me and I pounded harder, punishing myself regularly, as my true self became more and more immersed under the storm, at the source, because it simply was a fact I wanted no one to ever know I spent my entire life drowning, in shame and regret and guilt, for things I couldn't control, in the intention of making sure all around me were protected and safe, ensuring these storms were weather-able, and that was the way of the world, as I could make a difference for someone else as I had accepted and agreed I wasn't worthy of weathering the storms myself...

As I sit here, in my new world, a world I rose up to grasping onto the life preserver just before I surrendered to this life long belief, gasping for air, I realized this...

Wow... what the heck just happened yo...

As I was driving to work today this all started to materialize in my mind.

I have experienced major shifts in my life.

"Like Many, my spirit had been screaming for the coast, perhaps ironic since I had been submerged my entire life by what I most desired..."

As I sit here, comfortable, content, safe, and most importantly, humble and grateful, I reflect on how I imagined and witnessed in my mind how out of this relentless tsunami. I have somewhat graciously, and most definitely enthusiastically, rose up onto riding the wave, the wave that I watched continuously ravage everything around me, the wave I used to punish myself with, as I hid behind it...

I can't even sit here and think or feel anything less than this:

Contentment

Contentment in completely feeling that I am now returning to sync, envisioning myself as the tide, which rises, which reseeds, which can be turbulent and can be still, working with the elements that surround it, the moon, the sun , the storms, the calm, with gravity, with all that is this magnificent universe.

As my life continues to return to an extremely rewarding and now desirable routine, I wanted to share this with you all...

This life is still just as magnificent as the day I started this program with you all in January 25, 2019, just as magnificent as the day I walked out of my job, just as magnificent as the day my baby went to the hospital, as the day I flew to Houston, and the day I left Arizona in my 1988 VW Vanagon with my father following me...

"Everything has changed yet I experience contentment, and I'm comfortable within my body, I'm right with my soul."

I allowed myself to meet myself, to stop denying me of the things that feel right, I fell in love with myself, I truthfully found worthiness from within, my power comes from within, fueled by this magnificent experience that started 47 years ago.

I still cry in certain moments when I think of my daughters, my ex-wife, my ex girlfriend...

But today I breathe through these moments As I allow myself permission to feel and think and be who I am

I value every incline of pain I've experienced.

It's magnificent that my heart literally still hurts because it's been broken, but not by another, broken by my resistance to myself.

That delivers forgiveness and I honor my emotions.

I fell in love with myself in a time when I had 12 other people around me whom I've never met.

Who have had the courage to show up, to share, to cry and laugh with me, who have set boundaries, who have talked to me at midnight, who invited me to lunch as I traveled to a new state, who direct messaged me, to you all that trusted me during your journeys and allowed me a safe welcoming REAL encouraging space to be seen and heard.

"To all of you, I've been inspired and empowered and honored by you."

This has been the most magnificent moment of my life...

Because of our time and work to date I am content, still and calm in this moment, and I carry each of you with me as I experience "framing " my new world around all of our examples.

Refusing to accept anything less than the magnificence we've all shared together.

Cheers to these tears of life.

My family, I love you, thank you for allowing me to be a part of your lives.

In Magnificent Love and Light for us all always !

Eric.

JOURNAL YOUR THOUGHTS

YOU ARE LOVED

YOU ARE SAFE

YOU ARE FREE

"With Love and Light, Eric."

Made in the USA
Las Vegas, NV
14 September 2021

30249593R00062